Shite
Excuses

Find the excuse they haven't heard before

Moira la Chame

Crombie Jardine
PUBLISHING LIMITED

13 Nonsuch Walk, Cheam, Surrey, SM2 7LG
www.crombiejardine.com

Published by Crombie Jardine Publishing Limited
First edition, 2005

ISBN 1-905102-15-1

Designed by 'Mr Stiffy'
Printed & bound in the United Kingdom by
William Clowes Ltd, Beccles, Suffolk

CONTENTS

*He who cannot dance claims
the floor is uneven.*
- Hindu saying

*Don't make excuses,
make good.*
- Elbert Hubbard

INTRODUCTION

Some say we live in a 'culture of excuses' today. But if you think about it, we've been making excuses since we were first put on this earth:

God: Did you eat that apple I expressly told you not to?

Adam: It was Eve's fault, she gave it to me; you put her here with me anyway.

Eve: It was the snake's fault. He tricked me.

Ever since that snake set the trend, we've been having a devil of a time trying to wriggle out of things. Sometimes we are clever about it, sometimes witty, sometimes even believable. More often than not, though, our excuses are a poor disguise for our laziness, unwillingness, forgetfulness or plain guilty consciences. As a result, there are some really shite excuses doing the rounds!

If you must excuse yourself or others, and we all do, be original.

Many excuses are now so well used that they've become the stuff of legend and cliché and that policeman, your boss, partner, teacher . . . will probably have heard them before.

Pick yours with care!

The only man who is really free
is the one who can turn down
an invitation to dinner without
giving an excuse.
- Jules Renard

SHITE EXCUSES FOR GETTING OUT OF A DATE

My plot to take over the world is thickening.

I have to fulfil my potential.

My subconscious says no.

My mother would never let me hear the end of it.

You know how we psychos are.

It wouldn't be fair to the other Beautiful People if I went out with you.

I'm trying to be less popular.

The voices in my head are telling me to stay away from you.

SHITE EXCUSES FOR ENDING A SHITE DATE

I love cats, too.
How shall we cook yours?

My wife will be waiting up for me.

Can we talk in Klingon?

My other partner would
like to meet you.

I'm really looking for someone to
cook, clean, and iron my shirts.

I'm ovulating in an hour.

My other personality comes out at midnight.

You should know that the Viagra will wear off soon.

My husband is waiting at home for a threesome.

Would you like to see my train-spotting manual?

I think I'm a closet gay.

My wash cycle should be finished by now.

Would you like to see the tattoos I got in prison?

Will you marry me?

*It is better to offer no excuse
than a bad one.
- George Washington*

*He who excuses himself
accuses himself.
- Gabriel Meurier*

SHITE EXCUSES FOR MAKING IT A ONE-NIGHT STAND

I have to keep my appointment with God.

Did I spend the night with you? I'm jogging my memory, but nothing's coming up.

It wouldn't be fair to all the other girls/guys out there if I spent another night with you.

Off with the old, on with the new.

So many men/women, so little time.

Another day, another date.

Let's not spoil the memory of a perfect night.

I'm sorry but the clinic opens soon and I must keep my appointment.

I've consulted the voices and they say you're not the one.

> I read my palm and there wasn't a line for you and me at this juncture.
> — Anon

*Temptation is a woman's
weapon and a man's excuse.
- Henry Louis Mencken*

*An excuse is worse than a lie, for
an excuse is a lie guarded.
- Alexander Pope*

EXCUSES FOR SHITE SEX

I can't relax.

I have a headache.

This has never happened before.

I guess it's nature's way of
saying no hard feelings.

I knew I shouldn't have
given blood today.

I guess my pointer just turned
into a setter.

I'm sorry, but my store of fantasy

figures has run dry.

It's taking a power nap.

It's a cold night.

It prefers the South Pole to the North today.

It just doesn't like you.

EXCUSES FOR BREAKING UP

I need more time. Can you come back in thirty years?

I need some space – I need to see the moon.

I'm holding you back; you're driving me forward.

I can't see you anymore – I have a detached retina.

I'd love to grow old with you, but you're far too in front for me to catch up.

Ideological differences are no excuse for rudeness.
- Judith S. Marin

Several excuses are always less convincing than one.
- Aldous Huxley

And oftentimes excusing of a fault Doth make the fault the worse by the excuse.
– William Shakespeare

I will not take but for an answer.
– Langston Hughes

THAT'S THE TICKET

Since there are now no excuses that hold sway with traffic wardens and their ilk, even when you're in the right, here's a tale of a bloke who got away with being wrongfully parked.

A man went into a shop to buy a newspaper. When he came out a traffic warden was approaching. He went up to him and said, 'Come on, mate, how about giving a guy a break?' The warden ignored him and continued to walk up to the car parked outside the shop. The man called him a pencil-necked Nazi. The warden smiled and began writing a ticket. So the man called him a piece of horse shit. The warden continued to smile and placed the ticket on the windscreen. The man then crossed the road to a car parked on a double-yellow line, jumped in, and drove away.

If you don't want to
do something, one excuse
is as good as another.
– Yiddish proverb

Every vice has its excuse ready.
– Publilius Syrus

COP THAT, COPPER

Unwise things to say to a police officer . . .

I wasn't driving straight because your headlights were obscuring my view of the road.

I have insurance with Jesus Christ.

I heard you say pull over, but as I'm not wearing one I thought you meant some other guy in a red Ferrari.

I can't hand you my licence 'cos then

I'd have to put down my beer.

You must have been doing about 125 m.p.h to keep up with me! Don't you know that's speeding?!

Do you know why you pulled me over? Okay, so one of us does.

I was trying to keep up with traffic.

I was trying to get out of your way.

The earth is travelling round the sun at over a hundred thousand miles per hour: what's an extra thirty?

EXCUSE ME, OFFICER

A police officer stops a blonde for speeding and asks her very nicely if he could see her licence. She replies in a huff, "I wish you guys would get your act together. Just yesterday you take away my licence and then today you expect me to show it to you!"

These ones are true . . .

FIERY BLONDE

A pretty blonde was stopped for speeding late one evening.

"OK lady, where's the fire?" said the policeman.

"Oh, Officer, in your eyes!" she replied.

She got off with a warning.

RESTLESS MUM

A woman driver, eight months pregnant, whose existing two children were fighting in the back of the car, was stopped by a policeman wanting to check her road tax. The disk had actually expired the day before.

"I offer no excuse, officer, just take me to jail. I need the rest," she said.

To which the policeman replied, sympathetically, "Have a good day, Ma'am."

THE TROUBLE AND STRIFE

A fellow bought a new sports car and was out on the motorway for a nice evening drive. The top was down, the breeze was blowing through his hair and he decided to open her up.

As the needle jumped to 100 m.p.h, he suddenly saw a flashing blue light behind him and was pulled over.

The policeman came up to him, took his licence without a word, and examined it and the car. Finally he came back to

the window, looked steadily at
the driver and said, "I've had a tough
shift and this is my last pull over. I
don't feel like more paperwork so if
you can give me an excuse for your
driving that I haven't heard before,
you can go!"

The driver blinked only once while
his brain scrambled for a reply . . .
"Last week my wife ran off with a
cop," he said, "and I was afraid you
were trying to give her back!"

Justifying a fault doubles it.
— French proverb

Two wrongs don't make a right,
but they make a good excuse.
— Thomas Szasz

WAY TO GO . . .

As a pensioner was driving down the motorway, his car phone rang. Answering, he heard his wife's voice:

"Herman, I just heard on the news that there's a car going the wrong way on the M1. Please be careful!"

"SHITE!!" cried Herman, "It's not just one car. It's hundreds of them!"

DRIVE ON THEN

More true tales as told by a cop . . .

A police officer once pulled over a car driver in Detroit for going the wrong way down a one-way street. After talking to the driver, who was obviously intoxicated, the officer asked him if he saw the arrows. The driver replied, "I didn't even see the Indians . . ." Needless to say he found himself walking home.

THAT'S A FINE ONE

A policeman stopped a car that had gone through a red light at a major intersection. There had been plenty of time to stop, yet the vehicle had not even slowed down. The young female driver told him she had just had her brakes repaired, it had been very expensive, and she didn't want to wear them down. As the brakes were working fine, a fine is what this driver was awarded.

FAST THINKING

A female driver was stopped
for speeding and she had this
excuse to offer:

"A friend of mine told me that
this is a scary part of the road,
that BAD people live in this area.
I wanted to get through this area
as fast as I could!"

*Good taste is the excuse
I've always given for
leading such a bad life.
- Oscar Wilde*

*He that is good for making
excuses is seldom good for
anything else.
- Benjamin Franklin*

HANDY TIPS FOR GETTING RID OF A COPPER

* Feign an attack of diarrhoea.

* If male, say your wife is in hospital giving birth.

* Say you were choking on something and accidentally put your foot on the accelerator.

* You felt dizzy/had blurred vision so had to pull over in the no-stopping area, as it would have been dangerous for you to drive.

* Go into apology overdrive. Say sorry for everything you've ever done, from the way you drive to the fact you were ever born. Hopefully, the police will quickly tire of you and send you on your way.

* Affect a speech impediment. "I'm sssssssssssorry offfffffficer, but I didddnnnn't realize I was sssssssspeeding." Take your time over it and they wwwwon't ask you many further questions.

*Never ruin an apology
with an excuse.
- Kimberly Johnson*

*It is easier to find an excuse
than to find a reason.
- Doug Brown*

REAL SHITE EXCUSES FOR HAVING A PRANG

A pedestrian hit me and went under my car.

I collided with a stationary truck coming the other way.

I was taking my canary to the hospital. It got loose in the car and flew out the window. The next thing I saw was his rear end, and there was a crash.

Coming home, I drove into the wrong

house and collided with a tree
I don't have.

I had been shopping for plants all
day and was on my way home. As I
reached a junction, a hedge sprung
up, obscuring my vision.

I thought my window was down;
but found it was up when I put
my hand through it.

The pedestrian had no idea which
direction to go, so I ran over him.

I saw the slow-moving, sad-faced
old gentleman as he bounced off

the hood of my car.

To avoid hitting the bumper of the car in front, I struck the pedestrian.

In my attempt to kill a fly, I drove into a telephone pole.

I pulled away from the side of the road, glanced at my mother-in-law, and headed over the embankment.

I was sure the old fellow would never make it to the other side of the road when I struck him.

An invisible car came out of nowhere,

struck my vehicle, and vanished.

The accident occurred when
I was attempting to bring my car
out of a skid by steering it into the
other vehicle.

As I approached the intersection, a
stop sign suddenly appeared in a place
where no stop sign had ever appeared
before. I was unable to stop in time to
avoid the accident.

The telephone pole was approaching
fast. I was attempting to swerve out
of its path when it struck my front end.

The guy was all over the road. I had to swerve a number of times before I hit him.

A truck backed though my windshield and into my wife's face.

My car was legally parked as it backed into the other vehicle.

There aren't nearly enough crutches in the world for all the lame excuses.
- Marcus Stroup

DON'T GIVE ME THAT HORSESHIT

The General went out to find that none of his G.I.s were there. One finally ran up, panting heavily.

"Sorry, sir! I can explain, you see I had a date and it ran a little late. I ran to the bus but missed it, I hailed a cab but it broke down, found a farm, bought a horse but it dropped dead, ran 10 miles, and now I'm here."

The General was very skeptical about this explanation, but at least he was here so he let the G.I. go.

Moments later, eight more G.I.s came up to the General panting and he asked each of them individually why they were late.

"Sorry, sir! I had a date, it ran a little late. I ran to the bus but missed it, I hailed a cab but it broke down, found a farm, bought a horse but it dropped dead, ran 10 miles, and now I'm here."

The General eyed them all, feeling very skeptical, but since he'd let the first guy go, he let them go, too.

A tenth G.I. jogged up to the General, panting heavily. "Sorry, sir! I had a date and it ran a little late, I ran to the bus but missed it, I hailed a cab but . . ."

"Let me guess," the General interrupted, "it broke down."

"No," said the G.I., "There were so many dead horses in the road, it took forever to get around them."

SHITE EXCUSES FOR MISSING CHURCH ON SUNDAY

There are too many sinners in church.

I work six days a week.
The seventh day belongs to me.

Veni, Vidi, Non-Velcro.
(I came, I saw, I didn't stick around.)

Football is the new religion anyway.

Shopping malls are the new churches anyway.

I'm allergic to incense.

I did not miss church, in fact I had quite a good time shopping.

NO EXCUSE FOR MISSING CHURCH THIS SUNDAY

To make it possible for everyone to attend church this Sunday, we are going to have a special 'No Excuse Sunday':

Beds will be placed in the foyer for those who say, 'Sunday is my only day to sleep in.'

There will be a special section with lounge chairs for those who feel that our pews are too hard.

Eye drops will be available for those with tired eyes from watching TV late on Saturday night.

We will have steel helmets for those who say, 'The roof would cave in if I ever came to church.'

Blankets will be furnished for those who think the church is too cold, and fans for those who say it is too hot.

Scorecards will be available for those who wish to

list the hypocrites present.

Relatives and friends will be in attendance for those who can't go to church and cook lunch, too.

We will distribute 'Stamp Out Stewardship' buttons for those who feel the church is always asking for money.

One section will be devoted to trees and grass for those who like to seek God in nature.

Doctors and nurses will be in attendance for those who

plan to be sick on Sunday.

The sanctuary will be decorated with both Christmas poinsettias and Easter lilies for those who never have seen the church without them.

We will provide hearing aids for those who can't hear the preacher and cotton wool for those who think he's too loud!

See you on Sunday!

EXERCISE THAT EXCUSE

Nearly everyone knows exercise is good for you. However, most of us have a reason for not exercising as often as we should, if at all:

I am in shape. I'm round in shape.

My hair might get messed up.

My swimsuit might get wet.

I might sweat.

My husband gets jealous if I lose weight.

I don't want to give my mother the satisfaction of saying I'm taking care of myself.

The pool would empty if I dived in.

If I exercise I lose my appetite.

The gym is full of perverts.

The gym is full of thin people.

I wouldn't have enough energy left for sex.

Muscle weighs more than fat.

I'll lose weight first.

I don't have the time.

Gyms are too expensive.

It's too hot.

Exercise bores me.

Liposuction requires less effort.

Exercise makes you fat.

I'm on a Stress Level Elimination Exercise Plan: SLEEP!

WEIGHING UP
THE EXCUSES

It's my slow metabolism.

The diet starts tomorrow.

I hardly eat a thing.

Chocolate is good for you.

A little of what you fancy
doesn't do you any harm.

The cream puff had my
name written on it.

I just have to look at food to get fat.

SHITE EXCUSES FOR NOT GOING TO WORK

Scared to call the boss with an I'm-afraid-I-won't-be-in today? The people who came up with these excuses should have been . . . no doubt some of them are staying at home for good . . .

I have eye trouble and can't see myself working today.

The council is paving my street and I can't get out of the house.

My agoraphobia is kicking in.

My ergophobia (fear of work) is back.

My spirit guide says work
is for losers!

I'm all out of Prozac.

Constipation has made me a
walking time bomb.

My home computer has a virus and I
think I'm going down with it.

My car was repossessed while
I was asleep.

I've got car trouble. It's heading for
an amusement park and I'm in it.

I got ill on my golfing weekend, and do
not feel up to par today.

I need to get my wife pregnant.

I can't come in to work today because
of illness and fatigue.
I'm sick and tired of my job.

What is the good of being a genius if you cannot use it as an excuse for being unemployed?
- Gerald Barzan

IF YOU'RE A GIRL
WORKING FOR A GUY

Now come on girls, they've wised up to period pain so why not be more original . . .

I've sprained my uterus.

I have a nasty rash on my chest.

I've got a chapped clitoris.

I've got cystitis.

I've got PMT and can't stop crying.

I've got PMT and might kill you.

I've got thrush.

I'm having vaginal spasms.

I've got an infected nipple.

I've got mastitis.

I've had an allergic reaction to my bikini wax and can't put my knickers on.

I found my G-spot last night.

Just don't say you're ovulating or trying to get pregnant. However, once pregnant, feel free to have morning sickness, backache, fainting spells, spotting, cramp, and once the baby is born a spell of post-natal depression. However, if your child gets sick more than once, say that it is you and not the child who is ill. Bosses are a whole lot more understanding that way around.

IF YOU'RE A GUY WORKING FOR A GUY

I need time off to arrange a mortgage.

I need time off to look at a car.

I'm attending my son's sports day.

That beer must have been off.

I'm buying an engagement ring.

That was a really long business lunch so I'm going home now.

I have a stinking cold.

HANDY TIPS

* If you told your boss you sprained your ankle, when you return to work put a pebble in the shoe on that foot. That way you will not only remember which ankle you hurt, but by the end of the day you'll be limping for real.

* If you told your boss you had a headache, cold, cough or diarrhoea, take a packet of Anadin, bottle of syrup, Imodium or such like and leave said bottle/packet in view on top of your desk.

* If you want to be drastic, a little shampoo in your eyes will redden them nicely to substantiate your cold/eye-infection story.

* Go for detail, green and yellow puss, green and yellow poo, blood on your white trousers, shrimps and peas in the vomit. No one wants to hear this.

* By the way... have you ever noticed how when you pretend to have a stomach bug or flu, your colleagues mysteriously go down with it as well?

TELLING TALES

A woman in Florida was forced to call her office to say she would be late because she had a four-foot alligator in her driveway.

** **

A woman once called in to work from A&E. Running late for work she had tried to iron out the creases in her shirt while actually wearing it, and ended up with a serious burn.

EXCUSE ME?

In America, 3,400 mobile-phone users, mostly unknown to each other, formed an 'alibi-and-excuse club' to help each another skip work, get out of dates, have affairs and such like. When in need, each member can send out a help message, whereupon other members will invent plausible excuses or even ring bosses and wives.

Some have pretended to be doctors or policemen, authenticated by a sophisticated range of background noises.

HEY BOSS, I NOT COME WORK TODAY . . .

Hung Chow calls work and says, "Hey, boss I not come work today, I really sick. I got headache, stomach ache and my legs hurt." The boss says, "You know Hung Chow, I really need you today. When I feel like this I go to my wife and tell her to give me sex. That makes everything better and I can go to work. You try that." Two hours later Hung Chow calls again. "Boss, I do what you say and I feel great. I be at work soon. You got nice house."

THE BOSS BITES BACK

MEMORANDUM

TO: All Staff

FROML The Management

SUBJECT: Sick Leave Policy

SICKNESS:

No excuse... We will no longer accept your doctor's statement as proof. We believe that if you are able to go to the doctor, you are able to come to work.

AN OPERATION:

We are no longer allowing this
practice. We wish to discourage
any thoughts that you may need
an operation. We believe that as
long as you are an employee here,
you will need all of whatever you
have and should not consider having
anything removed. We hired you
as you are, and to have anything
removed would certainly make you
less than we bargained for.

DEATH:

Other than your own

This is no excuse for missing work. There is nothing you can do for them, and we are sure that someone else can attend to the arrangements. However, if the funeral can be held in the late afternoon, we will be glad to allow you to work through your lunch hour and subsequently let you leave 1 hour early, provided your share of the work is ahead enough to keep the job going in your absence.

Your own

This will be accepted as an excuse.
However, we require at least two
weeks' notice as we feel it is your
duty to train your replacement.

Signed

The Management.

THE GET-OUT-OF-SHITE EXCUSE FORM

(* delete as applicable)

Dear * Mom / Dad / Love of my life / Assistant Principal / Local Police Chief,

Words cannot begin to express how sorry I am that your * car / house / pet / espresso maker / left arm was severely damaged by my * infantile / puerile / inept / comically brilliant but nonetheless * sadistic / woefully under-appreciated prank. How could I have known that the * car / jet ski / large helium balloon / rodent-driven sledge / zamboni I was riding in would go so far out of control? And while it is true that I should not have pointed it in the direction of your * house / wife / Cub Scout troop / 1/16th-sized replica of the Statue of Liberty, complete with torch-light / priceless collection of Rolling Rock beer cans, you must understand that it was all meant in fun. The subsequent carnage that I caused is beyond my ability to * imagine / fathom / comprehend / appreciate / pay for. And I must therefore humbly ask your forgiveness. I know that you are perfectly within your rights to * hate me / sue me / spank me / take my firstborn / gouge out my eyes with spoons and feed them to the fish in your koi carp pond. But I ask you to remember all the good times we've had, joshing around at * school / work / church / the bowling alley / the municipal jail and to remember that I am first and foremost your * friend / child

/ sibling / lease co-signer / only possible match should you ever need a bone marrow transplant. I think that counts for more than one prank that * was so stupid / was so silly / would have been funny if it worked / you would have done if you had thought of it. Especially as I'm going to use it again on someone else.

Sincerely,

* the perpetrator / anonymous / me / [insert real name] / [insert someone else's name]

We are all manufacturers.
Making good, making trouble,
or making excuses.
- H. V. Adolt

HOW NOT TO GET OUT OF JURY SERVICE

A man was chosen for jury duty who really wanted to be dismissed from serving. He tried every excuse he could think of but none worked. On the day of the trial, he decided to give it one more shot. As the trial was about to begin, he asked if he could approach the bench.

"Your Honour," he said, "I must be excused from this trial because I am prejudiced against the defendant.

I took one look at the man in the blue suit with those beady eyes and that dishonest face and I said to myself, 'He's a crook! He's guilty!' So, your Honour, I cannot possibly stay on this jury!"

With a tired annoyance the judge replied, "Get back in the jury box, you fool. That man is the defendant's lawyer."

MY ARSE!

Two tigers are stalking through the jungle when the one in the rear suddenly sticks out his tongue and licks the butt of the one in front. The lead tiger turns and says, "Hey, cut it out." The other tiger excuses himself, saying he tripped on a tree root.

After about five minutes the rear tiger repeats his action. The front tiger turns angrily and says, "I said don't do that again!" The rear tiger says sorry, he was running from a snake.

After about another five minutes, the rear tiger repeats his action. The front tiger turns and says, "So what's the excuse this time?" The rear tiger says, "I'm really am sorry. The truth is I ate a lawyer this morning and I'm just trying to get the taste out of my mouth."

Whoever wants to be a judge
of human nature should study
people's excuses.
– Hebbel

I attribute my success to this:
I never gave or took an excuse.
– Florence Nightingale

DEAR SIR . . .

REAL SHITE REASONS GIVEN FOR NOT ATTENDING SCHOOL

Dear School, Please Eckuse John being absent on Jan 28, 29,30,31, 32 and also 33.

Please excuse Gloria from Jim today. She is administrating.

Please excuse Roland from P.E. for a few days. Yesterday he fell out of a tree and misplaced his hip.

John was absent yesterday because he had two teeth taken off his face.

Carlos was absent yesterday because he was playing football. He was hurt in the growing part.

Mary could not come to school because she has been bothered by very close veins.

Chris will not be in school 'cos he has an acre in his side.

Please excuse Pedro from being absent yesterday. He had ~~diahre dyrea dineathe~~ the shits.

Please excuse Jimmy for being. It was his father's fault.

Please excuse Jennifer for missing school yesterday. We forgot to get the Sunday paper off the porch, and when we found it Monday, we thought it was Sunday.

Sally won't be in school a week from Friday. We have to attend her funeral.

My daughter was absent yesterday because she was tired. She spent a weekend with the Marines.

Please excuse Jason for being absent

yesterday. He had a cold and could not breed well.

Please excuse Mary for being absent yesterday. She was in bed with gramps.

Please excuse Burma, she has been sick and under the doctor.

Maryann was absent December 11-16, because she had a fever, sore throat, headache and upset stomach. Her sister was also sick, fever and sore throat, her brother had a low grade fever and ached all over. I wasn't the best either, sore throat and fever. There must be something going around, her father even got hot last night.

Please excuse little Jimmy for not being in school yesterday. His father is gone and I could not get him ready because I was in bed with the doctor.

I'm sorry Tyler can't go to school today because his hormones are raging.

I CAN'T COME INTO SCHOOL TODAY . . .

Tommy (putting on his Dad's voice on the phone): "I'm sorry but Tommy can't come into school today."

Teacher: "Why?"

Tommy: "He has a terrible cold."

Teacher: "Who is this speaking?"

Tommy: "It's my Dad!!"

The absent are never
without fault, nor the
present without excuse.
- Benjamin Franklin

There are new words now that
excuse everybody. Give me the
good old days of heroes and
villains, the people you can bravo
or hiss. There was a truth to
them that all the slick credulity
of today cannot touch.
- Bette Davis

NO EXCUSE FOR SHITE GRAMMAR

A gentleman wanders around the campus of a college looking for the library. He approaches a student and asks, "Excuse me, young man. Would you be good enough to tell me where the library is at?"

The student, in a very arrogant and belittling tone, replied, "I'm sorry, sir, but at this establishment, we are taught that there is no excuse for ending a sentence with a preposition!"

The gentleman smiles, and in a very apologetic tone replies, "I beg your pardon. Please allow me to rephrase my question. Would you be good enough to tell me where the library is at, asshole?"

OH SHITE!

Two University students who spent the weekend partying rather than revising, failed to turn up for an exam on Monday. On Tuesday they were full of apologies and used their rehearsed excuse (that they had travelled to another county and were delayed driving home on Sunday night because their tyre blew in the middle of nowhere). However, they were still made to sit the test, in separate rooms. No doubt both found the test somewhat challenging – especially the last question: 'Which tyre?'

DON'T GIVE ME ANY SHITE

An English teacher reminded her class about the exam they had to sit the following day. She told her pupils that there would be no acceptable excuses for not showing up, except for serious injury, serious illness, or a death in the immediate family. At this point a smart-ass in the back of the room asked, "What about extreme sexual exhaustion?" The teacher smiled patiently and said sweetly, "Not an acceptable excuse. You can write with your other hand."

INFANTILE EXCUSES

My imaginary friend told me to do it.

It was the poltergeist.

If I'm so bad, you can't be
raising me right.

The big boys on the bus made me do it.

It's just what the babysitter said.

[To the babysitter] Mum and Dad
always let me stay up this late.

I took it because everyone
else has one.

It just happened. It broke itself.

It's glass, what did you think would happen to it?

There was an earth tremor.

I'm sorry but I did it on accident!

You should have put it somewhere safe if you valued it that much.

I do what the additives tell me.

It's not a mess – it's a statement.

I'm not farting – I'm just burping out my bum.

*How strange to use 'You
only live once' as an excuse
to throw it away.*
— Bill Copeland

MUM WON'T BUY THAT!

There was a really cute princess walking through the woods, and she heard a voice calling, "Hey Really Cute Princess!"

She looked around and didn't see anyone but a frog. She started to walk on but the frog called again. "Hey Really Cute Princess, if you take me home and let me sleep on your pillow, I will turn back into a Handsome Prince!"

It had been a very boring day so she decided to give it a try even though she really didn't believe the frog. The really cute princess took the frog home with her and let him sleep on her pillow. When she got up the next day what do you think she found? There on her pillow sat a really Handsome Prince.

Do you believe the story? Well neither did her mother!

THERE'S NO EXCUSE FOR THAT . . .

Farmer John has three sons. One day his oldest comes to him and pleads with him to get him a car. His father says, "Son, come with me!" He takes him to the barn and points to the farm tractor and says, "This here tractor is needed for the farm and I promise, as soon as it's paid for, we'll get you a car."

A week later, the second son approaches the farmer wanting a motorbike. Well, he gets the same excuse ". . . as soon as the tractor is paid for . . ."

Shortly after that, his youngest is bugging him for a bicycle. He too gets the lecture about the tractor needing to be paid for first.

While leaving the barn, the youngest boy sees the rooster mating with one of the hens, and promptly goes over and kicks it off the hen's back.

His dad says, "Son, why would you

do something like that? He didn't do anything to you. There's no excuse for that behaviour."

The little boy says, "Oh yes there is. You said no one rides anything around here until the tractor is paid for."

EXCUSES FOR NOT CALLING

I lost your number.

Didn't you get my note?

My telephone line was cut off.

I lost my voice.

I lost my phone.

I've been away.

I've been ill.

I must have left a message on the

wrong answer phone.

I thought it was your turn to call me.

I thought my colleague rang you back.

I had to keep my line free for an urgent call.

I painted my nails so couldn't dial the number.

You aren't my friend any more.

NO-WIN EXCUSES
FOR SHITE PLAY

Oh . . . have we started the real game?

You never said "Go"!

Who did we say was keeping score?

The sun was in my eyes.

I couldn't concentrate because you were giving me dirty looks.

The net was higher than usual.

My foot fell asleep.

There was a draft coming from somewhere.

Aren't we still rallying?

The floor slopes.

The pitch was uneven.

The lighting's not good in here.

This new racquet is pants.

My trainers have no grip on this floor.

*

EXCUSES FOR NOT SUCCEEDING IN LIFE

I belong to a long line of unfortunate people.

My parents didn't want me.

My parents didn't encourage me.

Fate has never been kind to me.

I wasn't born with a silver spoon in my mouth.

I was born during an eclipse - I've been eclipsed all my life.

It's in my genes.

I wasn't born lucky.

I'm a victim of both nature
and nurture.

I just didn't get the breaks I needed.

The government is to blame.

I don't get high, but sometimes I wish I did. That way, when I messed up in life I would have an excuse. But right now there's no rehab for stupidity.

– Chris Rock

'Very sorry can't come. Lie follows by post.'

- Telegram sent by Lord Charles Beresford to the Prince of Wales after an eleventh-hour summons to dine

If you really want
to do something, you
will find a way. If you
don't, you will find
an excuse.

-Anon

WHY WE'RE NOT INVITING YOU TO DINNER

I don't think you'd get on with these dreadful neighbours we're obliged to invite.

Didn't you get my invite?

We thought you were out of the country.

I'm sure you told me Derek was on a stag weekend.

Everyone else is vegetarian.

I only found your telephone number today and I know how hard it is for you to get a babysitter.

I'm such a crap cook, you'll be glad I've spared you.

Didn't I tell you we changed it to Sunday?

The children will be up till ten and I know just how much that will annoy you.

We're having sheep's eyes for starters, but do come if you want to.

That chap you had an affair with is coming.

We're looking after a cat and I know you're allergic to them.

That woman your husband has his eye on will be there.

We may have bird flu, but come if you want to.

GREEN EXCUSES

I have no interest in going green;
I'm not The Hulk

Some like it hot.

I like my vinegar on my chips not
on my windows.

My car says more about me
than a bicycle.

The world is going to end
soon anyway.

Global warning will cut my heating bills.

What's wrong with my greenhouse anyway?

The bottle bank is always full.

Organic food is too expensive.

I don't like the idea of food that you have to wash.

We don't get enough recycling bags.

*

Go on, excuse yourself!

THE END

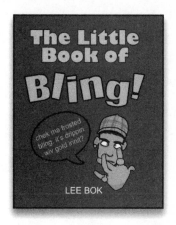

1-905102-21-6 • £2.99

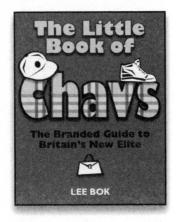

The Little Book of Chavs

The Branded Guide to Britain's New Elite

LEE BOK

1-905102-01-1 • £2.99

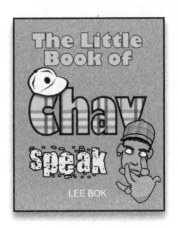

The Little Book of **Chav speak**

LEE BOK

1-905102-20-8 • £2.99

1-905102-26-7 • £2.99

The Little Book of-

GOTHS

Dan Vice

1-905102-24-0 • £2.99

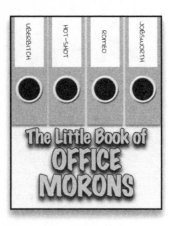

1-905102-28-3 • £2.99

the little eBay book

UNOFFICIAL   UNOFFICIAL

The website's most weird and wondrous...

1-905102-19-4 • £2.99

1-905102-14-3 • £2.99

All Crombie Jardine books are available from your High Street bookshops, Amazon, Littlehampton Book Services, or Bookpost (P.O.Box 29, Douglas, Isle of Man, IM99 1BQ. tel: 01624 677 237, email: bookshop@ enterprise.net. Free postage and packing within the UK).

www.crombiejardine.com